DUPLEX

Mike Nagel

autofocus books
Orlando, Florida

Praise for Duplex

"A miraculous combination of comedy and despair. I completely loved the book."

—**David Shields**, author of *Reality Hunger*

"'Things, I've noticed, are coming apart,' writes Mike Nagel. And: 'One way homicide detectives can tell a suspect is lying is if their story makes perfect sense.' If you, too, are looking for clues, my fellow detectives, then you should read *Duplex:* a pandemic-era chronicle in which, as things come apart, Nagel does something more important, more impressive and more difficult than making perfect sense: he tells you the truth."

—**J. D. Daniels**, author of *The Correspondence*

"I loved hanging out in Mike Nagel's *Duplex!* It was discombobulating in all the best ways. I look forward to seeing what he does next."

—**Amy Fusselman**, author of *Idiophone*

"I could write about the wending and winding perfect sentences, the way your brain hypnotically starts thinking a little differently while reading, but instead I just want you to know that I read this book straight through on a cross country flight, letting my body shake a little, chuckling to myself while holding in full-on, out-loud laugher like a dork, a possibly ideal reading experience—in distraction level, activity itself, and the pleasure of starting a perfectly short book in one location and finishing just a few hours later in another."

—**Aaron Burch,** author of *Year of the Buffalo*

Published by Autofocus Books
PO Box 560002
Orlando, Fl 32856
autofocuslit.com

Essay/Fiction
ISBN: 978-1-957392-00-4

Cover Illustration ©Amy Wheaton
Library of Congress Control Number: 2022930422

For J, obviously.

"Tenant must maintain appropriate levels of necessary chemicals."

—Paragraph 17, Section (5), Standard Duplex Lease Agreement in the State of Texas

"Where I am is called *here*."

—J.D. Daniels, *The Correspondence*

DUPLEX

The story goes that my family was once future heirs to the Jack in the Box empire. At the last minute my grandfather backed out of the deal and now I drive a used Nissan Sentra. I have no idea if this story is true, but it has always defined my life in reverse. I am living this life instead of that one.

"It's like all the sudden all anyone wants to do anymore is be locked in a small room and then try to escape from it," Matt says over drinks.

People will do almost anything to pass an hour. There seems to be no end to the number of things that will float our boats. What floats my boat is not leaving my house for days on end while polishing off a liter or two of vodka and not reading any of the books I've promised myself I'll read before I die. *The Brothers Karamazov.* The Rachel Cusk trilogy. The Warren Commission on the Assassination of President John F. Kennedy. I watch TV instead and make deals with myself about which activities will trigger the need to take a shower.

Recently my wife, J, and I moved into a duplex in the middle of nowhere. The cool thing about a duplex is the way it looks like one house on the outside but on the inside it's really two houses. That's the duplicity of the duplex. A welcome change from the complexity of the complex, where my wife and I lived in a fourth floor walkup the past five years. It's quiet out here in the middle of nowhere. Our appliances are all fifty years old, manufactured by General Electric. In the event of a nuclear disaster, we can crawl inside our washing machine. The oven has a setting for BEEF HAM, an animal I can only assume has since gone extinct. The clock is busted. In our kitchen it's always 7:34, sometime in the 1950s.

I got drunk the first night in the duplex and saw a cockroach on the kitchen counter. It hid behind the knife block. I understood its hiding to be an act of fear. That cockroaches are capable of feeling fear struck me as devastating proof of the deep sadness that permeates every level of THE GREAT CHAIN OF BEING. I smashed it with a spatula. Cockroaches, as you know, are full of motor oil. It went all over the place. "Free motor oil!" I yelled and wiped it up with a paper towel. Later I woke up on the couch, having not fallen asleep.

Lately this weird thing has been happening to me where

I wake up more often than I fall asleep. For example, I woke up three times yesterday but only fell asleep once. Similarly I am shitting constantly but hardly eating. A problem of my inputs and outputs, my starts and stops. Hardly anything adds up all the way. "If you eat a quarter pounder, you'll only gain a few ounces," a co-worker explained to me. Jodie says she gave birth to an eight-pound baby and lost five pounds.

Our neighbor in the duplex is an old fart named Iris. She's so old she might have seen an honest to god BEEF HAM. Our second day in the duplex, she rang our doorbell twice. That was the first time I heard our door-bell. It sounds like this: DING DONG! But when Iris rings it, it sounds like this: DING DONG! DING DONG! I hadn't been out of the duplex since I'd walked into it the day before.

"I've woken you," Iris said.

"No no no," I said, but then realized she had.

"Maybe we should exchange phone numbers," she said. "In case I'm ever being too loud." But I knew that she meant the opposite.

"Sure," I said.

"I live alone but I'm not lonely," she said.

"Okay," I said.

I wrote my number on a neon pink sticky note.

"Sometimes I play jazz at a low volume in the kitchen while I cook," she said.

I nodded and tried to remember why people tell

each other things, a line of thinking that, like all lines of thinking, eventually leads to killing yourself.

"Whatever floats your boat," I said.

"My boat?" she said.

"Your *boat*," I said and handed her the sticky.

Over July 4th weekend, J goes to Canada to visit her grandma so it's just me and Iris in this duplex with this thin wall between us. In the mornings I drink coffee on the couch and listen to Coltrane through the wall. That cat could really blow. Dead at forty from liver failure. There are, of course, *implications*. I stay home from work so I can focus on drinking, binge-watching a show starring Giovanni Ribisi, and arranging my books into various piles around the living room. Before bed, I look at my car in the garage and briefly but vividly suicidally ideate. I don't take showers. I don't sleep well. I dream about cockroaches. The exterminator told J they live in the trees. "Why would he tell you that?" I say. "Why would he think that was something anybody would want to know?"

I'm not escaping the room. The room is the escape. I have McDonald's delivered. A twenty-piece box of chicken nuggets costs the same as a ten-piece box of chicken nuggets. A large Coke costs the same as a small Coke. The economics of Mickey D's astound. It is not possible to order just one pie. "I've woken you," the delivery guy says when he passes the box of nuggets to me through a gap in the door. "No no no," I say, rubbing my eyes, waving him away.

I text my dad.

 Me: Is it true that Grandpa Leo was almost a founder of Jack in the Box?

 Dad: It's true. He turned it down. We coulda been rich!

Our new city is in a dry county which means I have to drive fifteen minutes in any direction if I'm going to buy booze. You can tell where the county line is because of all the liquor stores. I wait in line with three liters of vodka under my arms while the guy in front of me asks for the smallest bottle of Jack they have. The clerk hands him the size you'd get on an airplane.

 "What's one bigger than that?" the guy says.

 "A pint," the clerk says.

 "What's one bigger than a pint?" the guy says.

 "A fifth," the guy says.

 "A fifth of what?" the guy says.

 "A gallon," the clerk says.

 "I'll just go ahead and take the gallon," the guy says.

I heard once that if you know what time the liquor store closes you're a person who likes to drink, but if you know what time the liquor store opens you're an alcoholic. After I heard that, I was very careful to not find out what time the liquor store opens.

Our new neighborhood seems quiet enough, but just to be safe I drive to Academy Sports on a Saturday morning and buy a bat. A child-sized Louisville Slugger. The adult-size costs $109, but I think the $34 child-size will do just as good a job at bashing in someone's skull. I stand in the aisle and take a few over-the-head practice swings. I wonder if it's obvious that I'm picturing braining an intruder. To confuse any potential suspicion about my intentions for the bat, I also buy a pack of racquetballs. I am disguising myself as a person who does not understand which pieces of sports equipment go together. When I get home I drink vodka and beat the shit out of a plastic trash can the previous tenant left in the garage.

J gets home from Canada late Sunday evening and I wake up on the couch. "I've woken you," she says. "No no no," I say. Then I say a bunch of other things I don't remember saying. Not remembering saying them, I feel the need to say them again. As many times as it takes. I tell J about my bat. "Do you want to see it?" I say. And she says, "I'm worried about you." At thirty-two, I seem to be experiencing early-stage symptoms of dementia and late-stage symptoms of existential dread. A potentially deadly combo. I wake up every morning at 3am sweating. *Am I doing it wrong?!* I think, about my whole life.

I like to imagine that things were simpler in the 1950s when this duplex was built and my grandfather was passing up the opportunity of a lifetime—the opportunity of multiple lifetimes—and we still didn't know that the moon is nothing but a big stupid dust ball of disappointment. Men and women thought they knew what each other were for. The mighty BEEF HAM was roaming the Dallas suburbs, grazing on bluebonnets and discarded Whataburger fries. Unfamous people were on the cover of *People* magazine. Sex from behind had yet to be discovered.

I resolve to get healthy. "Both of body," I say to myself, "and of mind." The double whammy. The triple whammy includes finances but I'm not sure I have any of those. I buy a salad at Starbucks. It costs ten fucking dollars. There's quinoa in it. That's healthy! Maybe it's the quinoa that empowers me that night to lucidly dream. I do what I always do in a lucid dream. I run around like crazy trying to have sex with as many people as possible before I wake up. Thank you, lucid dreams! Thank you, quinoa!

I get a text message. For the purposes of this essay let's say it's from Iris.

Her: Random question...but I've been doing some research as a result of some therapy I've been doing because boy am I feeling just generally misunderstood and out of place. Do you ever feel like that?"

Me: Constantly, my entire life.

Her: How do you fight the urge to just like...become a hermit and never interact with the outside world?

Me: Haha. Not fighting that urge very well tbh. How about you.

Her: It's not going well.

When we find a lawn mower in the garage, I pretend to not know what it is. "Maybe it's for digging holes," I say. "Maybe it's art."

My parents call at nine thirty one night "just to say hi" so I guess people are starting to worry. I haven't been seen in nearly a month. "We've woken you," they say when I answer. I happen to be sober at the time so I make a point of acting REALLY SUPER SOBER by staying on topic and not immediately forgetting everything I say. I can tell they're impressed. I sound great. Healthy of mind and body. I might visit New York. "New York!" they say.

The fifth cockroach I find is dead already of what appears to be natural causes. My dog bit its head off. "And that makes five," I say. When the exterminator comes for the second time he says, "That's a problem" and points to all the dishes I haven't done.

"Don't bring me problems," I say. "Bring me solutions."

"What do you think this is?" he says and holds up the canister he's been carrying.

"I don't know," I say. "Something poisonous, I hope."

"Damn right it's poisonous," he says.

When he's done spraying he says, "Wait, you don't have kids, do you?"

Nobody tries to break in. Nobody tries to break out. The bat seems to be working. Sometimes when J's gone I get naked and hold the bat to my crotch like it's a giant penis and walk around the duplex wagging it around. I don't know why I do that. You know what, forget I mentioned it.

I am offered a lucrative freelance opportunity writing a script to stroke the egos of the most powerful CEOs in the world. Men and women who knowingly or un- knowingly CONTROL THE INVISIBLE HAND. "Someone's got to bring home the BEEF HAM," I tell J. I take the job and utterly botch it. "What is this?" the marketing director says about the twenty pages of incoherent nihilistic ranting I turn in, carefully for- matted in A/V. For this failure I am paid half the agreed upon amount, enough to cover one month's rent at the duplex.

I used to think I was going to make my living as a suc- cessful writer. Now I make my living as an unsuccessful one. Our lives are just whatever's left over after everything else doesn't work out. Reasons to drink abound. Nothing else in the history of maritime has floated more boats. But be warned: whatever it is that floats your boat is also the thing in which you might drown.

After three days without showering my face gets shiny. I start to smell. A musty animal smell that I neither like nor dislike but somewhat intoxicates me. The primal smell of the BEEF HAM. My psoriasis clears up a little. My hair looks great.

Our neighbors on the other side play Mariachi music at night. The bass line travels into our duplex via underground pipes. It comes up through the drains. There is only one Mariachi song. I don't know what it's called but it's very sad. "Play it again!" I yell down the drain when it goes quiet, sometime around nine thirty.

Per city ordinance, on Wednesday nights I take the trash can to the end of the driveway. All the empty bottles inside rattle. "Shhhhh!" I say. I don't know about you but it's taking more and more to keep my boat afloat. My boat is heavy and poorly designed. My boat is named THE U.S.S. LIVER FAILURE. With all this drinking I've been doing you'd think I'd be better at the saxophone. "But what about the God-shaped hole in you?" a friend asked me once in an attempt to *lure me back into The Kingdom*. "That's the great thing about vodka,"

I explained. "It can conform to any shape."

Has it started yet? I sometimes think, about my life. And sometimes, *Is it over yet?*

J and I fly to New York in the middle of a heat wave. It's a hundred degrees in Central Park. We take taxis just for the air conditioning. "Twice around the block," we say. We act like we're the rich heirs of a fast-food empire. We put it on the card for future versions of ourselves to worry about. *They'll know what to do*, I think. I have great confidence in them.

On the second night we walk the High Line and eat cantaloupe-flavored gelato. Then we visit a sex shop called The Blue Room in what J calls The Gayborhood. "No returns," the old man behind the counter says when we walk in, a row of fat rubber penises behind him arranged like a skyline. "Check New York City sex shop off the list," J says after we leave. "List?" I say. "What list? Was I supposed to be keeping a list?"

I don't blame my grandfather for his almost complete lack of balls. A restaurant called JACK IN THE BOX doesn't exactly sound like a safe bet, especially for a man not particularly inclined to gamble. My dad once told me that my grandfather is the type of man who started planning for his retirement at age twenty-one and started collecting pension on his sixty-sixth birthday.

Now he plays tennis in Arizona and doesn't come to our weddings.

When we got back from New York J and I met with a financial advisor who told us that at our age and income level we should have $215,000 in savings. I laughed so hard I got the hiccups.

On Monday night I water the lawn. Fifteen minutes per section until it turns into mud. When the whole lawn is mud, you're done watering the lawn. I hire a neighbor kid to mow once a week for $20. My first employee. A simultaneous product of my protestant work ethic and my late-stage American laziness.

"Come anytime," I tell him. "And don't feel any pressure to do a great job or anything."

"You're so *suburban*!" J says when I tell her about hiring the kid.

A week later I fire him. He's useless and unreliable.

"We've decided to go in another direction with the position," I text him, then let the grass grow and grow.

It's March 2020. There are mayflies everywhere. They must have come early this year. Or maybe they're just poorly named. "Who *named* these things?" I say to no one, swatting another away from my bedside light. They fly around like they have no idea how to fly and can't believe what they're doing is actually working. They die on contact. They're super fragile. They're made of mud and cotton candy. Most people don't know that.

When you smash a mayfly nothing happens. It's anticlimactic. Surprise. There's nothing inside. Like an empty Wonder Ball. I guess I mean a ball.

Like everyone else in the world, I'm home waiting out the spread of the virus, seeing who gets it, seeing if I get it, seeing what happens to all of us when we all eventually get it. Probably the worst. It's a fantastic time to be a pessimist. "So many situations and people to assume the worst about!" I tell J. "I almost can't decide!"

Once a day I walk around my neighborhood to keep the blood from pooling in my heart. According to my most recent blood work I am 85% chicken nugget.

I walk past the police station, through the frisbee golf park, then over to the pond. I listen to Run the Jewels, The National, Small Black, Bleachers, in that order. I keep my mouth shut. If I didn't keep my mouth shut I would eat about a hundred mayflies. They would fly directly into my mouth and dissolve. They would taste like mud and cotton candy. I thought about buying a 3M brand N95 series COVID-19 edition mask just to keep the mayflies out of my mouth but everyone else beat me to it.

"It was a good idea and you beat me to it," I say to everyone else as I walk past them at the pond. I'm not shy about calling out a great idea when I see one and this was a great idea.

[]

An executive order comes down from the mayor's office. "Everyone is hereby ordered to stay home for the foreseeable future."

There is, of course, no such thing as the foreseeable future.

There might not even be such thing as the future.

"Should we go ahead and pretend to take this seriously?" a reporter at the press conference asks.

"Great question," the mayor says. "Yes. Everyone is hereby ordered to go ahead and pretend to take this seriously."

[]

"What am I supposed to be, like, *getting out of this?*" I say to J as we start our second week at home.

"I think the point is what you're supposed to *not* be getting out of this," she says.

"Well it's working," I say, "because I'm not getting *anything* out of this."

I still think everything happens for my education. You'd think I'd know better by now. But I don't.

[]

When I was a kid somebody told me that mayflies are the most poisonous bugs on earth. Their fangs are just too small to bite us. I have no idea if that's true. Probably not. Very few things are true. But I've gone on believing it anyway. I'll believe anything anybody tells me about bugs. I do very little research. Let's call it none.

Still though. After accidentally swallowing a mayfly near the pond, I wonder if maybe it's time for me to start doing a little *due diligence* in terms of my understanding of the Animal Kingdom. I ask J about it. She's getting her PhD in being right about everything all the time. She's almost done with her coursework.

"I ate a mayfly three days ago," I say. "What can you tell me?"

"Mayflies prevent the spread of algae, contribute to

local nutrient cycling, *and* hunt mosquitos for sport. We need as many of them around as possible," she says. "You really should try not to eat them."

[]

This year I'm celebrating my tenth anniversary of believing that we're all alone in the big dumb empty universe.

Before I believed that we're all alone in the big empty universe, I believed that we *weren't* all alone in it. I believed in God! That was nice. I'm not trying to be condescending. I'm being condescending on accident.

It's not particularly special to believe in God. Most people do. And it's not particularly special to not believe in God. Most people don't. There is, I suspect, a lot of overlap.

Honestly, though, the subject of God and whether or not he/she does/doesn't exist bores me to death.

To *death*.

And I wouldn't have even brought it up if I didn't suspect it is somehow, inexplicably, inextricably, *fundamentally* related to The Point.

[]

First the mayflies, then the June bugs. They hurl themselves against the windows at night. I guess they're trying to get in. In the morning I find them dead on the patio.

"Failure!" I say.

I go around pointing at each one individually.

"Failure! Failure! Failure!"

I don't know what the June bugs are doing out so early but here they are.

"It's March," I say. "*March*."

Last week I saw a TED Talk.

"As I'm sure you know," the talk began, "we are living in the Sixth Extinction of Life as We Know It on Planet Earth."

"Actually, for your information, I *didn't* know that," I said to the TED Talk. "And, to be honest with you, I really feel like I should have been told."

On second thought it made sense.

On third thought I *did* know that we are living in the Sixth Extinction of Life as We Know It on Planet Earth. I'd just forgotten. I'm super forgetful. There are a lot of things to remember and it's hard to remember all of them at once. I should really start writing some of them down.

Now that I remember that we are living in the Sixth Extinction of Life as We Know It on Planet Earth, I remember something else: I have no idea what I am supposed to do with that information. I never know what to do with information. I don't know what information is for. What's the point of knowing things? I just walk around all the time nodding and smiling like, "Uh huh, uh huh, yep, this all makes sense, sure, why not."

[]

Thursday evening I go for my walk and Iris is sitting there with two ducks in her front lawn. They have big green heads. They're swimming around in a Rubbermaid container the size of a rollaboard suitcase. Ducks are capable of swimming around in really small circles. That's just a little duck information for you. You probably won't need it.

"Are these *your* ducks?" I say.

"They're just passing through," Iris says. "They're late this year."

"Are you sure they're not early this year?" I say. "A lot of things are early this year."

"Nope," Iris says. "Late."

[]

So. I don't know. Sometimes it's almost like there's not even a theme.

[]

I'm not going to lie it's a little scary being all alone in the big empty universe. Sometimes I get a stomachache just thinking about it. It's almost like anything can happen at any moment and there might not even be some sort of takeaway.

Like how in high school I knew this kid named Todd. He had absolutely nothing going for him, Todd. Not talented. Not good-looking. Not funny. Not smart. Not well-liked. Not anything. I'm not trying to be mean. These are facts.

Facts.

Anyway. Halfway through Todd's freshman year of college he dropped dead of a brain aneurism. They found him on his dorm room floor. They checked. Definitely dead.

"Well what was the point of *that*?" I said when I found out he'd died.

Or like how one day in Downtown Dallas I watched a man jump off the building next to mine. He landed in front of the 7-Eleven.

"Ummmmmmmmmmmmm," I said.

[]

"Uuuuuuuuuuuuuuuuuuuuuuuuuuuuummmmmmmmmm mmmmmmmmmmmmmmmmmmmmmmmmmmmmmmmmmmmm mmmmmmmmmmmmmmmmmmmmmmmmmmmm," I continued to say, sort of under my breath, for the next five and a half years until it was kind of a Zen thing.

[]

An executive order comes down from the mayor's office. "All non-essential businesses are hereby closed until further notice."

It's nice, at least, I think, *to finally know what's essential.*

When it comes to the day-to-day functioning of this operation very few of us are what you would call ES-SENTIAL PERSONNEL. In a pinch, the world could continue basically as-is with a skeleton crew of one hundred fifty mildly competent ninth-graders. The rest of us are just bonus. We should try to remember that.

[]

When I notice my tan getting uneven, I decide to start walking in the opposite direction.

"It's time," I announce to J, "to turn things around."

I walk to the pond. Then through the Frisbee golf park. Then past the police station. I listen to Bleachers, Small Black, The National, Run the Jewels, in that order. I smile at people. I turn on the charm.

When the sun starts setting, the light catches the mayflies just right and they glow. They look like they're battery powered or something. They look like they're made out of fiberoptic cable and LEDs. I do some quick math. There are one hundred billion of them.

"Buncha drunks!" I say. "Sober up, you fucken bun-cha drunks!"

And then, against my will, I start thinking about that stupid Coldplay song, the one where he says that we live in a beautiful world.

Coldplay? I think. *At a time like this?*

And I try to think about another song—a better song—I really do, but I can't think of any other song, so I just keep on walking around thinking about that dumb Coldplay song. I think it's called "Don't Panic."

I was trying, and failing, to meditate away a hangover. I'd heard that this could be done. The source was unreliable. It's possible that I was the source. I can't always remember what things other people have told me and what things I have told myself. The problem, I think, is that I am great to tell things to. People are always telling me things, myself included. I don't know what I'm supposed to do with the information. The hangover— the result of a normal enough night of drinking—was *ab*normal in its ability to completely obliterate my desire to go on living what Frederick Exley calls, in his 1968 fictional memoir *A Fan's Notes*, "that long malaise, my life." It was, as we say in the testicle community, A REAL KICK IN THE BALLS. This happened to my balls sometimes: a normal enough night of drinking kicked me in them. I hated to say it but I was starting to wonder what the point of drinking even *was*. I had done so much of it, had invested myself in it so thoroughly, for so long, and *this* is what I get? Kicked in the balls? To be fair to drinking, my balls weren't exactly *precious cargo.* Some hidden defect or childhood damage had rendered them practically useless in The Child-making Department. I could fuck okay. There just wasn't any good reason to. At least not one of any use to our species as a whole. Luckily, considering our inability to have children, or maybe *because* of our inability to have children, J and I had stopped wanting them. It might be human nature to want things you can't have but it's also human nature to *just kind of get over it at some point already.* Our decision to not have kids—to not even *want* kids—was both a huge relief and a major burden. Now that we didn't have to worry about having kids, what would we worry about? We all have to worry about something. Sometimes I think it's *what we're here to do.* I poured myself a drink and thought it over. Then I poured myself another drink and kept thinking it over. The more I thought the more I drank until it became a little hard to tell what I was doing exactly: thinking or drinking. By my early thirties, always thinking or drinking, I had begun to resemble the main character of Fredrick Exley's 1968 fictional memoir *A Fan's Notes*, a character (presumably Exley) who, in his early thirties, is always thinking or drinking. *How relatable!* I read the book continuously and so was always thinking or drinking or thinking about thinking and drinking. There was, it seemed to me, a lot to think about. *And*, it seemed to me, a lot to *drink* about. In fact there seemed to be an equal number of both. Exactly one to one. That almost never happened! It would be unreasonable, I reasoned, to think about something without drinking about it afterwards. And it would be unthinkable, I thought, to drink about something without thinking about it first. *Besides*, I thought and reasoned, *look at Exley!*

I mean, *look* at him: By thirty-six, despite or because of all his thinking and drinking, Exley had still managed to publish what can only be considered an enduring piece of canonical loser-lit. Lesson being: a good book can make up for a lot of bad things, especially if the book is *about* those bad things, and Exley's, of course, was about those bad things.

Okay, now look away: because by sixty-three Exley, who had continued thinking and drinking, had thought and drank himself to death. That happens sometimes. The hazards of thinking and drinking abound. It was something to think about. And because it was some-thing to think about, it was also something to drink about. And so I thought about it and drank about it well into my thirty-second year despite or because of the tragi-heroic life of late American loser-writer Fred-erick Exley, dead at sixty-two of thinking and drinking.

Now that I was in my thirties, perhaps even *well* into them, I wondered if it might be time to reevaluate my role models. Most of them—writer-, artist-, musi-cian-types of the Exleian self-destructive bent—had died untimely deaths and lived unseemly lives. That was all well and good for them, I guessed, but proved some-thing of a problem for me as I was, generally speaking, a timely, seemly person. I shopped at Costco. I drank

SmartWater. It might be human nature to want to be someone you're not but it is also human nature to eventually *just sort of accidentally end up being someone you are*. In my case: a thirty-two-year-old childless duplex tenant with a bad hangover. It was an accident! I was trying not to think about it. I'd heard—or had told myself—that if I could just not think about it long enough that my hangover might go away. This, as far as I understood, was what meditating *was*: just not thinking about things. And, because you're not thinking about things, not drinking about them either. A double negative: not-thinking and not-drinking. *Easy!* I didn't do things all the time. I was practically a LEADING WORLD-EXPERT at not doing things. When I looked back at that long thirty-two-year malaise that had been my life, it was mostly me not doing things. Look: Here's me in Long Beach, not doing things. Look: Here I am in Dallas, not doing things. Oh look: I'm in West Africa, not getting anything done. *Finally*, I thought, *my superhuman capacity for inactivity is going to serve a narrative purpose.* I put MY SPECIAL LITTLE TALENT to work right away by continuing to lay there not doing anything. It didn't seem to be working. *Maybe*, I thought, *this is one of those situations where you have to give it a minute.* Sometimes you have to give things a minute. A minute is a metaphor. It means *a little longer than you were expecting.* A minute can be a minute or a minute can be sixty-two years. Minutes are really weird like that. And so I laid there and I gave it a minute. And when that minute was over, I gave it another minute.

And when that minute was over, you get the picture. The picture is of me laying there, giving it a minute. It was the least I could do. It was the most I could do. The least I could do was the most I could manage. I hoped I was still in some sort of *grace period*. I'd been meaning to find out who to call about that.

All of my problems were real problems. But some of my problems were only in my head. I went to see a dentist. Sexy Dr. Swenson on Josey Lane. It had been eleven years since I'd been to the dentist. Except, of course, it had been thirteen.

"According to our records you've missed your last twenty-seven appointments."

"Yah," I said. "Something came up."

While sexy Dr. Swenson went to work with her drill, I watched home renovation shows on HGTV. Sarah and Todd were on a tight budget but a breakfast nook was non-negotiable. They would have to sacrifice their ten-minute commute.

At the end of the day, these shows are all about *compromise*.

When sexy Dr. Swenson began drilling my front teeth, I realized I should have been *paying a little more attention* when she explained what needed to be done.

[]

Good morning! It's 7:34am on Tuesday, August 4, 2020, and I'm writing to you from sunny Carrollton, Texas, a little town outside of Dallas that I assume was founded by Carol. I would like to take this opportunity to say, "Thanks, Carol! Nice town!"

Nobody has ever heard of Carrollton. I've barely heard of it. And I live here.

The most famous person to come from Carrollton is the shitty white rapper Vanilla Ice. He went to high school at R. L. Turner, not far from where I'm writing this now. Vanilla Ice described his time in Carrollton this way: "I was in Miami."

As part of our duplex rental agreement, it's our job to keep the lawn alive. If the lawn dies, we have to buy a new lawn. I don't know how much a lawn costs. $30 seems reasonable.

[]

In June I turned 33. In August J turned 36. Like you, I'm a little surprised how quickly my life is going by. I have tentative plans to change the air filter in our HVAC system. It doesn't seem pressing.

"Once every three months," the guy said.

"What if I wait longer than that?"

"That's probably okay," he said.

"What if I wait a lot longer than that?"

"That's probably okay too," he said.

"What if I never change it the entire time we live

here?"

"Honestly," he said. "It doesn't really matter."

One interesting thing I've noticed about life is that our actions don't seem to have consequences.

"For every action there is an equal and opposite reaction," Sir Isaac Newton said in 1686.

I would like to say now, in 2020, to Sir Isaac Newton: "No there isn't."

[]

I was surprised, after moving to Carrollton, namesake of Carol, secret hometown of Vanilla Ice, how quickly I felt at home here.

"Why is that surprising?" J said.

"I guess I just thought I'd feel at home somewhere else," I said. "Like New York. Or Mexico."

On the weekends I go to the grocery store. They're having a special. Buy two bananas.

"What happens if I buy two bananas?" I ask the guy.

"Nothing," he says. "Just please buy two bananas."

Sometimes when I'm at the grocery store, I pick up a few things for Iris. Here's yesterday's list:

1 zucchini

1 pint of sour cream

1 slice of cake

I don't think it's productive to feel sad about other people's lives so I just leave the groceries on her front porch and tell her how much she owes me. She writes me a check. I don't know what to do with checks. I give them to J. I don't know what happens after that.

Iris and I are both watching our sodium for some reason. She texts me low-sodium salad dressing recipes, usually at 4am. She tells me about No Salt. It's just like regular salt except there isn't any salt in it.

It's possible, I've noticed, to have it all.

Sometimes Iris calls me up and we chat for a while. Turns out she's a fucken nutjob. Trump supporter. Conspiracy thinker. The whole thing. Last week she sent me an article: "Hydroxychloroquine Cures Type 2 Diabetes."

It's almost like you have to decide: Do you want to like people? Or do you want to get to know them?

"Had too many avocados," Iris texted me last night. "Left one in your mailbox :)"

[]

At night, J works on her PhD in our little makeshift office and I sit on our back patio reading *The Brother's Karamazov;* Rachel Cusk trilogy; the Warren Commission on the Assassination of President John F. Kennedy.

Someone said to write the books you want to read.

Okay, I think. But first I'm going to *read* the books I want to read.

"I am," I tell myself about this part of my life, "getting my reading done."

[]

Before sexy Dr. Swenson glued two new crowns into my mouth, porcelain replicas of my drilled-away teeth (upper back, stage left) I asked if I could see them. They came in a little plastic case. It looked just like the one I put my baby teeth in after they fell out twenty-some years ago.

"So...what? You, like, order them from some guy and he makes them in a shop and then he sends them to you in the mail through like FedEx and then you glue them into my mouth?" I said.

"Yep," she said. "That's how it happens."

"Oh," I said. "That's weird."

[]

The other night I ran into Iris out front while I was un-tangling the hoses. In this heat, you're supposed to water three or four times a week. I'd missed the last eighteen to twenty-four waterings. The grass seemed okay though. A little crunchy.

"I forgot to tell you," Iris said. "Try adding vinegar to the salad dressing."

"Vinegar," I said.

"Yeah," she said. "For some pop."

"Pop," I said.

It's a little surprising, I think sometimes, that I happen to be living this particular life in this particular place and not, for example, a different life someplace else. A community college professor in Florida, let's say. Or the heir to a fast-food empire in LA. Not that my life is bad. Just that the odds were against it.

[]

After three visits to the dentist over the course of a month, getting various teeth drilled out and filled in by Dr. Swenson, who I no longer consider very sexy, not very sexy at all, I walked across the hall to the dental hygienist, a middle-aged woman named Janet.

"I've cleaned the teeth of the most beautiful people in New York," Janet told me.

"And now you're doing it here in Carrollton," I said.

"Where?" she said.

[]

Books pile up around the duplex. They look like stalactites. Or stalagmites. Whichever one is correct.

The cat tries to jump on top of them. He's getting old though. And he was never a great jumper. Usually he just knocks the books over and I threaten to kick him out of the duplex.

At night we all sleep together in the big bed. A California king someone gave J and I as a wedding present. That was ten years ago now. Except, of course, it was more like twelve.

"I think it might be time to buy a new mattress," J says just when I'm finally starting to get used to this one.

"I'll let you in on a little secret about all these mattresses," a mattress salesman told me once years ago, and I am telling you now. "They're all exactly the same."

[**M**onday] Me and the pest control guy are standing in the front yard while he points at my duplex and tells me what's wrong with it. For one thing, something's been trying to gnaw its way inside. Probably a squirrel, he says. Maybe a rat. I choose to hear squirrel. I don't know why I'm more comfortable with the idea of a squirrel living in our attic. I almost welcome it. He points out the evidence while I pretend that what he's saying makes sense to me.

"See that separation between the shingles and the siding?" he says.

"Yep," I say.

"And those gnaw marks just above the eave?"

"Mmhmm," I say.

I'm full grown, happily married, gainfully employed, and sometimes I feel like my entire life is spent pretending to understand what's going on and just hoping it all makes sense later. It never makes sense later and it never seems to matter. A double mystery then. What's going on? And was it really necessary?

"Something might be living in our attic," I tell J when she gets back from the grocery store that afternoon. She's unloading groceries in the kitchen, including a large quantity of alcohol, which you have to go to a separate store for here in Texas, I guess to make sure you really want it.

"*Some*thing?" she says.

"Probably a squirrel," I say.

"Oh," she says. "I'm fine with that."

"Me too," I say, putting an entire Fruit Rollup into my mouth. "I just wanted to make sure we're on the same page."

She holds up a jug of Monopolowa vodka. She presents it like I've just won a gameshow.

"Jesus," I say. "A *gallon?*"

I can't remember whose idea it was but since we don't have any plans for Thanksgiving this year, we've decided to spend the week being drunk off our asses. Drunksgiving, J calls it.

"Do you think we should do something about it?" J says later that night. We're laying in bed, a little buzzed but nothing crazy, nothing *nutso*, nothing we're going to regret too bad the next morning. J's playing a game on Nintendo called *Animal Crossing*. You make a new home for a bunch of animals on an island. They walk around like people and have these huge heads. They speak this gobbledygook language that sounds like a dial up modem on helium. I've been watching her play it for hours and there doesn't seem to be a point to any of it.

"Something about what?" I say.

"Something about the thing that might be living in our attic," she says.

"Oh," I say. It literally hadn't occurred to me that we should do anything about it. Sometimes I forget that we can do things about our problems. Usually I just leave things alone until I forget about them or they become unbearable.

"Maybe we could call somebody," I offer.

"Who do you call about something like this?" she says.

I think for a minute. "Maybe we could call the police."

[**Tuesday**] I read a news story the other day saying a rare-metal asteroid is heading toward Earth that's worth an estimated ten thousand quadrillion dollars. The Dow Jones Industrial Average just hit thirty thousand for the first time in history. Next week the McRib returns to McDonald's franchises nationwide after an eight-year absence. "The Wait," the press release tells us, "Is Over." I can't help noticing that many of our frowns are finally turning upside down. "Congratulations," Twitter tells me when I log in for the first time in three months. "You have been randomly selected to take a survey."

I wake up slightly hungover but not bad. There are many types of hangovers. I don't mind telling you that I am something of an expert on each and every one of them. This is the one that feels like you're a tuning fork vibrating at 256hz. A hangover that lives mainly in the teeth and bones. I eat some leftover cauliflower-crust margherita pizza and drink some cold lime-flavored Topo Chico and pull my beanie down low onto my head. None of it helps, of course, but it still feels nice to take care of myself like this. The only real cure I know for a hangover is to start drinking again as soon as possible, but that's a dangerous remedy. I should know. I once spent years curing and creating hangovers that way, a mobius strip of pain and pain-relief, one becoming the other, back and forth, until it was a little hard to remember which one was causing which. I've heard that many talented deep-sea divers have lost their lives thinking they were swimming toward the surface when really they were swimming deeper into the abyss. They say if you are ever buried alive in an avalanche, the first thing you should do is hock a loogie, then dig in the opposite direction.

"They're coming on Monday to take care of the squirrels," J announces Tuesday afternoon.

"I thought we agreed that we were okay with the squirrels," I say.

"No," she says. "We were kidding. We can't have squirrels living in our house."

"I know that," I say. But what I mean is that I know that *now*.

I have to do a little work this week so I can't start drinking at 10am or anything. I have to wait a little. I write junk mail for a big fat financial company out by the airport. The things I write are sent out monthly by the millions. A New York Times bestselling novel only has to sell five thousand copies.

"How do you feel about the fact that we make garbage for a living," I once asked Lucy, the woman who puts the things I write into Adobe InDesign.

"Don't be negative," Lucy said. "Some people recycle."

Writing junk mail is exactly as easy as you think it would be. A mildly competent ninth-grader could do my job. A computer program could do my job. One is. Recently we hired a computer program. It writes terribly and gets spectacular results, three or four times better than anything I've ever written. I've heard we're paying it a million dollars a year.

"Yeah," I say, "but can it do this?" and then I do the little dance move I know that's all in the hips. I call it THE MIDNIGHT SPECIAL.

After I write my junk mail letters, after I *get my work done*, I throw back two or three shots of vodka in the kitchen, then one more shot of vodka, then I take an Angry Orchard apple cider and Michael Herr's Vietnam book, *Dispatches,* out to the patio swing. The cat follows me out there and hops up next to me. Like ten seconds later there's a loud crash somewhere in the duplex, near the garage. The cat and I look at each other, then look toward the garage, then look back at each other, then both decide that whatever it was doesn't require our immediate attention and we more or less get on with our lives. I don't know how we're supposed to know what does and does not require our attention. Every moment of every day is a triage situation unless you're willing to ignore a few things.

At night, after a few more ciders and a few more vodkas, and then a few more and a few more, as I'm lying on the couch watching *Interstellar* on my laptop, the duplex starts to *spin.*

[**Wednesday**] I couldn't tell you what the Vietnam War was about if my life depended on it. I watched three parts of Ken Burns's ten-part documentary, and I watched a heck of a lot of *Apocalypse Now*, and I watched all of *Forrest Gump* twice, and now I'm reading this *Dispatches* book, which is very good and all, very *interesting*, but after all that I *still* don't know what we were doing over there or what was going on or what the point of it all was.

One thing I've learned after all these years of writing

junk mail is that you have to get to the point early. And then you have to repeat the point again every two or three sentences. And then you have to put the point in a big, bold font. And even then 98.2% of people still won't get the point. I'm not sure if, in real life, there is even such thing as a point. Not a naturally occurring one anyway.

I've heard that one way homicide detectives can tell a suspect is lying is if their story makes perfect sense.

"Um, Mister," J says on Wednesday afternoon. I follow her out to the garage where the ceiling has fallen and broken all over the tops of our cars. Through the hole where the ceiling used to be, I can see the roof beams in the attic. A bunch of light is coming through. I guess there are a bunch of holes in the roof. They say that in art the imperfections are where god gets in. But in duplexes the imperfections are where squirrels and rats and bugs get in.

"What did you do?" I say.

"What did *I* do?"

"That's the opposite of where the ceiling is supposed to be," I say.

"I thought something looked weird about it," she says.

"You got the ceiling and the floor mixed up," I say.

"I see that now."

"The ceiling goes there," I say, pointing up.

She nods.

"And the floor goes *there*," I say, pointing down.

She nods again.

"And where does this go?" she says, giving me an unspeakable gesture that I won't describe for you here, but feel free to use your imagination.

After we stare at the hole in the ceiling for a minute, wondering how it got there, wondering if it has something to do with the squirrels, or something to do with the rats, or maybe something to do with something else—wondering, generally speaking, what things have to do with each other—we decide we should probably call somebody about this. Todd from maintenance will be here on Monday between nine and one.

"Does she have good bones at least?" I'll ask Todd after he has a look around our place, which has a hole in the ceiling now and squirrels in the attic and a funny smell coming out of the sinks that I didn't tell you about earlier because it didn't seem relevant at the time.

"No," Todd will say. "She doesn't."

[Thursday] Despite our best intentions to ignore our families this holiday season, we end up at J's parents' on Thanksgiving, I guess on account of the fact that we're all going to die someday. We sit at separate tables in the backyard and yell at each other through our face masks.

"If I get this virus, my business will go under," J's dad shouts at us.

"Don't worry," I shout back at him, "There's an asteroid heading toward Earth worth ten thousand quadrillion dollars. Money's about to not be an issue any-more."

"Are you kidding?" he shouts at me.

"I honestly can't tell anymore," I shout back.

For dinner, J's mom makes rouladen. It's beef stuffed with a pickle. Or maybe it's a pickle wrapped in beef.

"What," I shout. "No BEEF HAM?"

"What?" J's mom shouts back.

"No *BEEF HAM*?!" I shout back.

We stay until we have to pee.

"Well," we say when we have to pee, "that's our cue."

[**Friday**] In the morning my hangover is the one that feels like you've been beaten into a corner the night before during an amateur prize fight in some beer-reeking basement. A real working over, felt primarily in the solar plexus and balls. In his boxing book, *A Neutral Corner*, A. J. Liebling says of the nineteenth century boxer Abraham Belasco: "He could give but not take punishment." I know how Abraham felt. In this case I am the one giving the punishment, *and* I am the one not taking it very well. I spend Friday afternoon immobile on the couch reading *Dispatches* and drinking Topo Chico. This, it seems, is what I'm doing with my one wild and precious Friday afternoon.

"How we spend our days is, of course, how we spend our lives," Annie Dillard says in her book *The Writing Life*.

To which I say: "Uh oh."

"I drank myself into this," I announce to J that afternoon when my hangover still hasn't gone away, has somehow gotten worse. "My only option is to drink my way out."

"That doesn't make any sense," J says.

"Nothing true has ever made sense," I say, unscrewing the cap of the gallon vodka jug, now almost empty. "Ask a homicide detective."

"Seriously, where are you getting your information?" J says.

"NPR," I say. "Plus a little bit by making stuff up."

"You're ridiculous you know that," she says.

"Does this change your mind?" I say, and do a little dance, the one with my hips.

"The Midnight Special doesn't change minds," J says. "That's not what we *designed* it for."

A few seconds later the vodka kicks in and my head starts to sparkle and the light in the duplex changes somehow, it's hard to explain, softens up a little, and for a little while all my decisions become good ones; past, present, and future.

"See?" I say. But it's hours later by then, and I've just woken up on the couch, my head filled with the white cotton fluff of an oncoming hangover, my breath all hot and vodka-y—"like mustard gas and roses," Vonnegut says in *Slaughterhouse Five*—the *tck tck tck* of J's Nintendo controller coming from the other room.

On New Year's Day the Marines announce they will be issuing silencers to troops around the world. The wars will continue but they're going to try to keep it down. I'm at the grocery store buying more wine. I need more wine for a thing I'm doing later. The thing I'm doing later is drinking more wine. I put six bottles of Yellowtail merlot onto the checkout conveyor belt and they wobble their way toward the lady. $5 a bottle. 12.5% alcohol by volume, same as me. I stopped drinking last year but I also kind of *didn't* stop drinking last year if you know what I mean. I'm still drinking. That's what I mean. I should have just said that. Before I leave the store I see a kid wandering around the produce section wearing a pair of gun range ear muffs and wonder what he knows that I don't. Recently on Wikipedia I read about a new type of ballistic missile that hits first and then you hear it coming. It's called *Perseus*, after the guy who chopped off Medusa's head.

I'm drinking Yellowtail merlot on the back patio of our duplex on New Year's Day evening when the explosions start. Pops and thuds from over by the senior center. A sound like an advancing army and they're not being very sneaky about it. "Are those gunshots?" J says, poking her head out the back door. Hazards of the south abound. Last New Year's, Emily found a bullet hole in the roof of her Camry. Falling bullets are slow and silent but just as capable of blowing your brains out. Most victims are dead before they know they've been hit. It bothers me to think they might never find out. J and I sit on the porch swing passing the wine bottle back and forth. When it gets dark we can see the fireworks over the trees. First they flash, then we hear the pop. A disconnect of the audio visual. Things, I've noticed, are coming apart. Things, *I've noticed*, weren't all that put together to begin with. In the flash of each firework, we can see the leftover images of the fireworks before it. One hundred silent explosions burned into the sky. All of them grey and drooping and floating off toward Downtown Dallas. It looks like someone tried to erase them but did a bad job. It looks like that time I accidentally left my dad's old computer monitor on for too long and then there was a permanent ghost-image of a poorly played game of solitaire on the screen. A premonition after the fact. A harbinger in retrospect. They say if you hear a Perseus missile coming that means you *survived.*

After the temperature in Dallas drops into single digits, then the low single digits, before finally reaching a temperature of *one*, by far the most sarcastic temperature we've ever had as long as I've been here, the mayor declares a state of emergency. He goes on the news.

"It's an emergency," he says.

I look outside. I want to know what an emergency looks like. It seems like something that would be good to know. Something to *file away for later*. But when I look out there everything looks normal. A little blue.

It seems to me that the goal of life—one of the goals—is to stay alive as long as possible. I can't always remember why. In case something surprising happens, I guess. Our first night in a state of emergency a pipe in our bathroom freezes. I'm not too worried about it. We have plenty of pipes. This duplex is full of them.

"File this under Unintentional Learning Experiences," J says.

"That's where I file *everything*," I say. "You're going to have to be more specific."

"Okay," she says. "File this under Unintentional Learning Experiences *in the Bathroom*."

"Again," I say. "A fairly crowded category at this point."

As a Canadian, J has access to all sorts of cold-weather information not readily available to those of us in the lower forty-eight. She tucks her shirt into her pants and her pants into her socks. I wasn't supposed to tell you that.

When J was a kid up in Ontario she made an igloo. On Saturday, when the rolling blackouts start, I tell her that she might have to make another one.

"And I should tell you now," I say. "I have an extremely high standard of living. Be ready for feedback."

So. *Two* igloos, we decide. Two igloos would be best. Igloo neighbors. His and hers igloos. Left side, right side. Matchy matchy.

This year I'll turn thirty-four. J will turn thirty-seven. The cat will turn ten and the dog will turn six. There's a can of soup in our pantry that will turn two.

From everything I've read and seen and heard and *filed away for later*, it's only a matter of time before something really bad happens to all of us. It's totally normal, I'm told. *Happens to everyone.* "As if the horror of Death were not precisely its platitude!" Barthes says in *Camera Lucida*. Kind of yells it, actually.

At night we let the faucets drip. It sounds like we're sleeping in the hull of a sinking ship. I thought it was going to drive me insane. Instead I kind of like it. This is what has been missing from my sleep life. The threat of death at sea.

She's going down!, I think and drift off to sleep no problem.

I hear reports of people dying in the cold. A woman frozen to death outside a 7-Eleven. A mother and daughter dead inside their car. They say if you listen close you can hear pipes bursting. It sounds like this. *Tink tink tink tink tink.* On Thursday Greg comes over to fill mixing bowls with water.

"The store was out of buckets," he says.

I can't help noticing that this is getting a little ridiculous.

Is it just me, I think, *or is this getting ridiculous?*

The mayor goes on the news.

"It's ridiculous," he says.

J and I live next to a fire station, not far from a senior center, just down the street from a high school.

"Your duplex must be on a protected grid," Greg says when our power and water keep running long after his have shut off. It's always nice to be reminded that we are special, one-of-a-kind people who are never going to die. On Friday I make soup.

"What is this?" J says.

"Soup," I say.

"But what kind?" she says.

"There are *kinds*?" I say.

When the snow melts off the roofs it sounds like it's raining outside. As opposed to raining *inside*, I guess, where it sometimes rains too. We're advised to find our wrench. It's the wrench-shaped one. An elderly woman is found frozen to death inside her home. Other people too. An eight-year-old. People get electricity bills for $16,000. People don't have $16,000. Where are people supposed to get $16,000? We're told it could take years to figure out who to blame for this, and then a few more years to figure out what to blame them for. The mayor goes on the news.

"We're looking into it," he says.

They're looking into it, I think.

"We're demanding answers," the mayor says.

They're not asking, I think. *They're demanding.*

In the meantime there's work to do. There are pipes to re-pipe. Roofs to re-roof. Buckets to re-make and re-distribute and re-shelf and re-purchase. A mass-restoration of the GREAT SUPPLY CHAIN OF BEING. J says the only thing more destructive than the freeze is the thaw. All those burst pipes flowing and flooding. All those invisible problems bubbling up to the surface.

After a few days above freezing, dark splotches appear on our patio concrete, weird stains grow on our walls, something keeps dripping at night up in the attic, an infinite flow, a *renewable resource*, a potential solution to the world's water problems if someone could just figure out where the hell it's coming from.

It's getting warm again. At night the air conditioner runs. This duplex isn't sealed up very well. This duplex is kind of a shithole. It was built in 1953. A real low point for duplexes. The HVAC guy comes to check whatever needs checking and tells me that we're basically living in a worse-case scenario HVAC-wise.

"Uh oh," I say.

"Calm down," he says. "Be a man about it."

He walks around with his hands on his hips, shaking his head. His disappointment is obvious. It seems we could have been doing a better job at whatever it was we were supposed to be doing. He wipes some dust off a shelf with his fingers.

"*Pets?*" he says.

In *Speedboat,* Renata Adler says that when you live in the city anyone can call your life into question. But I live in a small town and it's the same thing here. At any moment you can be revealed to be a person who doesn't know what's going on. It's a risky business even picking up the phone. It could be anyone calling. Lately I've been getting calls from a number that looks like mine. The person calling could be me.

"Why do you keep calling me?" they say when I answer.

"I haven't been calling *you*," I say. "*You've* been calling *me*."

I get the feeling we're both being scammed. But for what purpose? And at what loss? *How is this even a viable business model*, I'd like to know? It seems the scams have gone art house. They're all 501c(3).

"There's a sucker at every poker table," Matt tells me. "I never know who it is so I always know it's me."

Our ceilings are too high. Our ducts are too small. There is no room to expand the ducts. They'd have to knock out the bedroom wall. They'd have to *get creative*. Our ceiling fan, I find out, has been spinning in the wrong direction.

"Anything else?" I ask the HVAC guy.

"Yeah," he says. "I know you haven't been changing the filter."

"We have been changing the filter," I say.

"Listen," he says. "It's cool. You don't have to lie to me. I'm on your team."

"We've been changing it," I say.

"If you lie to me I can't help you," he says.

"Every month," I say. "Like clockwork."

"Don't think of this as an *inspection*," he says. "Think of it as *a collaboration*."

Lacking much else by way of plot, I watch the weather for rising and falling action. A few months ago it was all falling. Now it's all rising. The weather is a George Saunders short story. Over time, the weather is a George Saunders short story *collection*. The grass seems to be turning green again. The leaves are coming back. It's almost tempting to see some sort of pattern in all of it. I said *almost*.

"I think sanity is the most profound moral option of our time," Renata Adler says. But that was fifty years ago. Fifty years ago *and counting*.

During the day it gets up into the 80s. The air conditioner runs constantly and inefficiently. Eleven cents per kilowatt hour. Cooling down the neighborhood. A drain on natural and unnatural resources. I've heard the most environmentally devastating concept ever invented was human comfort. A close second was the atomic bomb.

At night we drink Topo Chico on the patio and complain about our jobs. They're so much *work*, these jobs. They're so *demanding*. While we talk the dog hunts around the backyard for squirrels. Last night he found a snakeskin in the grass. It occurs to me that a house that lets so much out could also let things *in*.

The light fades and then we're sitting in the dark. Our next-door neighbor starts grilling something on his driveway. He listens to mariachi music and turns on his car headlights. Glowing white smoke floats up over the fence like a mushroom cloud. Later our whole place smells like brisket and hot sauce and I have some mariachi tune stuck in my head but don't know any of the words.

The spirit was willing but the flesh was weak. And to be honest the spirit wasn't all that willing. The spirit was tired. The spirit was thirty-four years old. A double weakness then. Spirit *and* flesh. In the evening, Iris texts to see if I can come over and dump the water out of her dehumidifier. After two years I've come to think of Iris as our house twin. Everything we have she has too but the other way around. Our kitchen is on the right and hers is on the left. Our patio is on the left and hers is on the right. We run a humidifier; she runs a *de*humidifier. Somewhere out there somebody is undoing all your hard work.

"I've just had dental surgery," she says. "The front door is open."

I walk over in my socks.

"Ding dong," I say into her house, my anti-house. "Knock knock."

[]

It's been a rainy summer. Week after week of storms.

Carrollton has finally gone tropical. "Lazy weather," J calls it. "Stay at home weather." Cloudy with a chance of Netflix. Any excuse to not leave the house. Not that I could go anywhere. My car's dead. A Nissan Sentra I've had since I was twenty-three. It's just sitting out there in the garage. The registration a year out of date. Dust on the tires. I hadn't been driving it. Then it became undriveable. It had sat there too long. Cars aren't supposed to sit there too long. Cars are supposed to drive around. If you don't drive them around, they stop driving around. A tautology. A self-generating argument. A perpetual motion machine. Or, in this case, a perpetual *non*-motion machine. The only way to make my car drivable again, I think, is to start driving it again, but I can't drive it because it's undrivable.

"Hmmm," I think.

[]

These are our last days in the duplex. We've rented an overpriced house in Plano, hometown of disgraced bike rider Lance Armstrong, Barney the Dinosaur, and the Frito Lay Corporation. The whole city smells like Doritos and economic entitlement. In the nineties it became kind of famous when a bunch of fucked up rich kids overdosed on black tar heroin. J grew up there. She says her high school was nicknamed "The Pharmacy."

We've been packing up the duplex, putting things into boxes, wiping things off with bleach and 409. I scrub out the oven. It's caked with remnants of every meal that's been made in it since 1953, since the days of the BEEF HAM. I scrape all that dried up crap into a trash bag and take it out to the curb. The goal is to make it look like we were never here. If we can make it look like we were never here, we get our deposit back. $1,500. One month's rent.

I fill in the holes in the walls with Aquafresh. I saw it on YouTube. You stuff Aquafresh into the holes with a butter knife. They disappear, kind of. It's magic, *kind of.* All of life requires some willing suspension of disbelief. It's not easy considering how unbelievable everything is. No matter what it is, I can never believe it. "Unbelievable," I say, about everything. I've heard that, mathematically speaking, we probably don't even exist. When I'm done the duplex smells minty fresh, cavity free, enhanced with 3D WHITENENING TECHNOLOGY and fluoride.

I look around.

"Whatever," I say.

[]

Monday morning I call a tow truck company about my dead Nissan.

"What's the nature of the issue?" the dispatcher says.

"Tautological," I say.

Hank shows up between one and three. He says he's seen this before. Someone doesn't go somewhere. Then they just keep on not going anywhere. It's pretty common. Especially these days. I ride up front with him over to Firestone on Josey Lane. We're way high up, bouncing around.

"Beep beep," Hank says as we squeeze through traffic. "Honk honk."

While we drive he tells me about his son, Mark, a tow truck driver in Seattle.

A family of tow truck drivers, I think. *Cool.*

Mark specializes in towing Teslas.

"Teslas are just one big battery," Hank says. "You tow one the wrong way, you get electrocuted opening your front door."

"That's interesting, Hank," I say. "But I drive a *Nissan*."

"You mean you *don't* drive a Nissan," Hank says, looking behind us at my dead car.

"That's correct, Hank," I say. "A Nissan is the type of car I *don't* drive."

We pass Albertsons. We pass Braum's. We pass Gabby's Chicken and Seafood.

"CLUCK CLUCK," the signs says. "SAVE A BUCK."

[]

My genius writer friend John says that doing too many drugs when you're young can lead to an overdeveloped sense of metaphor. "A poetical mind." If that's true

Plano should be chock full of Ashberys and Dickinsons. All those drugged up rich kids full grown and dried out and scribbling into Moleskines. I tell John not to worry. I didn't do drugs until I was in my late twenties. And I've never understood a single poem in my entire life.

"I wonder what this poem is about," I think about every single poem.

On Thursday I get a call from Firestone. They want to know how long I let my car sit there. They're interested for academic reasons. They're car scholars. The oil has turned to tar, they say. The gasoline has evaporated. The tires are now squares.

"Okay now give me the good news," I say.

"Good news?" they say.

[]

This next house will be the fifth place J and I have lived in together.

The first two times we moved, we moved closer and closer to the city. The next two times, we moved farther and farther away. Now we're right back where we started, in East Plano, just a few blocks from our first apartment. It took us ten years but we finally finished a lap around the DFW Metroplex.

We already have the keys to our new place so some days we just bring over a lamp or something. A shelf. A stack of books. A box of whatever. Some days we don't bring anything over.

"Not today," we say on those days.

No matter how many things we bring over there are always a few more things to bring over. An asymptotic exit strategy. Always leaving but never really gone. At night we sit on the patio of the duplex and drink wine out of a box. We listen to mariachi music from next door while the dog makes his rounds, diligent and suspicious, checking out every little thing.

[]

At some point I must have accidentally grown fond of this place. North Texas, Carrollton, our half-house on Jackson Circle, by the McDonalds. I don't know how it happened. You can grow fond of anything, I guess. I once asked a therapist how to be happier with my life. She said, "Have you tried lowering your standards?"

[]

On the last day of our lease, J and I lock ourselves out of the duplex with a few of our things still inside. We stand there for a minute. Then we say, "Ummmmmmmmmm."

We wanted to get out of this place. Now the only way out is back in. It feels like a Zen thing. Some stupid poem. "Un*believable*," I say. We call a locksmith. Big Pete off Keller Springs.

"What's the nature of the issue," Big Pete says.

"We think it might be a Zen thing," we say. "Possibly a poem."

"Are the doors locked?" he says

"Yes, Big Pete," we say.

"How locked are they?" Big Pete says.

"*Really* locked," we say.

"And the garage door?" he says.

"Closed," we say.

"And the power?" he says.

"Out," we say.

"Hmmm," Big Pete says. "Are you willing to do what it takes?"

"Probably not," we say.

[]

None of the things I worry about happen. The worrying seems to be working. It takes Big Pete about three seconds to get inside the duplex. He jiggles something and the door opens.

"That easy?" I say.

"That easy," he says.

"The whole time?" I say.

And he says, "Huh?"

It's late now. The power has already been disconnected. J and I work in the dark, cleaning up the last evidence that, for a while, this is where we lived. I Swiffer the floors. I Swiffer the countertops. I Swiffer the sinks. You can Swiffer anything. Some people don't agree. At some point we hear something creeping around outside. I look through the peep hole and there's Iris ringing the doorbell. The power's out though so there's not the usual DING DONG DING DONG. There's just *tck tck, tck tck.*

I'm not really in the mood to talk to Iris right now because I'm never in the mood to talk to Iris. Iris is nuts. So J and I just stand there freeze-tag style and eventually Iris puts a note in our mailbox and shuffles away. When we read the note later it'll say: "Thanks for being my friends for a while." It really will say that. All the sad parts of this book are true.

We clean quietly so Iris can't hear us through the walls. We creep around like a couple of sneaks. We can't really see what we're doing so it seems like we're doing a pretty good job. A few months later we'll get a de-posit-return check for $12.

I open a cupboard and find a bottle of wine. And behind that bottle of wine, a few more bottles of wine. Here's something I've noticed about wine. There's a lot of it. Eight thousand years of this stuff and we've hardly made a dent. We don't have any glasses so we drink straight out of the bottle like a couple of goddam rock stars. Next door, Iris is playing jazz music at a low volume. On the other side, our neighbor is playing mariachi music at a high volume. Everything, I've noticed, is cancelling everything else out. Nothing, I've noticed, is adding all the way up. The duplex creaks and groans, expanding and contracting, always settling, never set-tled. We pass the bottle back and forth. It sloshes around. There's something making scratchy sounds above us. Looking for a way in, I guess. Or maybe looking for a way out. We choose not to hear it. It's easy. We've been choosing not to hear things in this place for two and a half years. Hearing things is *optional*.

I open another bottle.

It goes: *POP*.

The sound above us grows louder, getting impatient.

"Don't worry," I say quietly to J, "we're going to get to the bottom of this," then throw my head back and tilt the bottle straight up toward the ceiling.

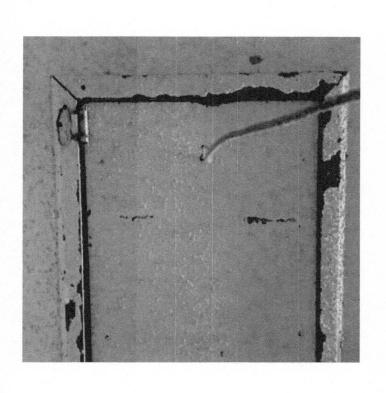

Acknowledgments

Parts of this book originally appeared in *The Hunger*, *No Contact*, *Hobart*, and *Little Engines*.

Huge thank you to the early readers of this thing: Matt Brown, John Daniels, and Kristen Ploetz. Also thanks to the fantastic lit mag editors who believed in some of these pieces early on: Lena Ziegler, Erin Slaughter, Gauraa Shekhar, Elliot Alpern, Laura Gill, and Adam Voith. Of course this book wouldn't exist without the amazing team at Autofocus, Michael Wheaton and Amy Wheaton. I can't thank you two enough for such a great experience putting this thing together. And finally to J, my all-time favorite person, thanks for everything.

About the Author

Mike Nagel's essays have appeared in apt, Hobart, Split Lip, Salt Hill, DIAGRAM, and elsewhere around the internet. He lives in Plano, Texas.